I0467608

Ultimate Guide To Animal Tattoos

Everything You Need to Know About Animal Tattoos

Animal Tattoo

By : Gala Publication

2

Published By :

Gala Publication
© Copyright 2015 – Gala Publication

ISBN-13: **978-1522707059**
ISBN-10: **1522707050**

Table of Contents

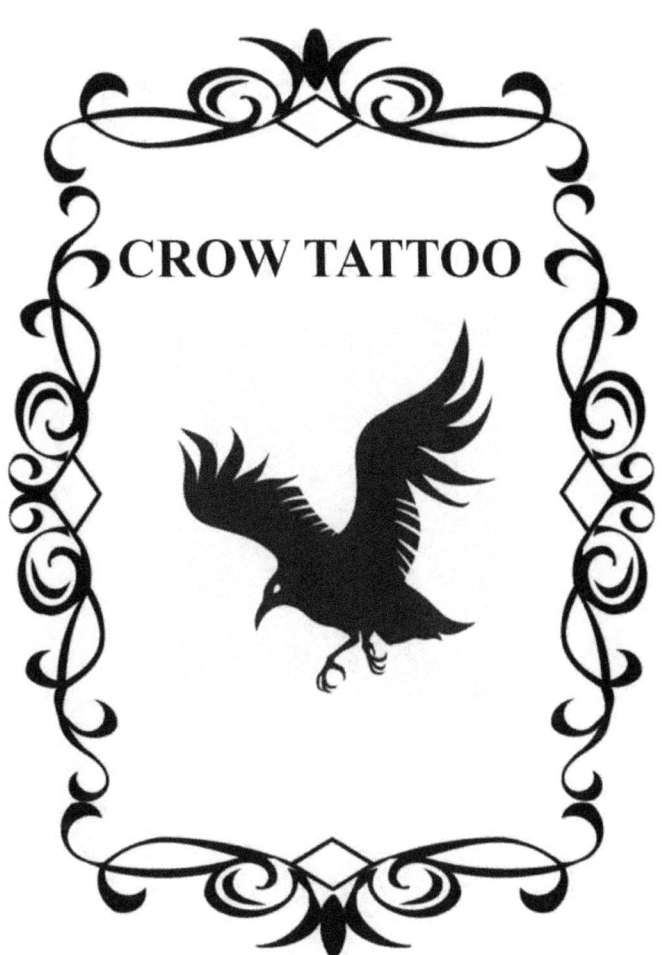

CROW TATTOO

STEP 1

STEP 2

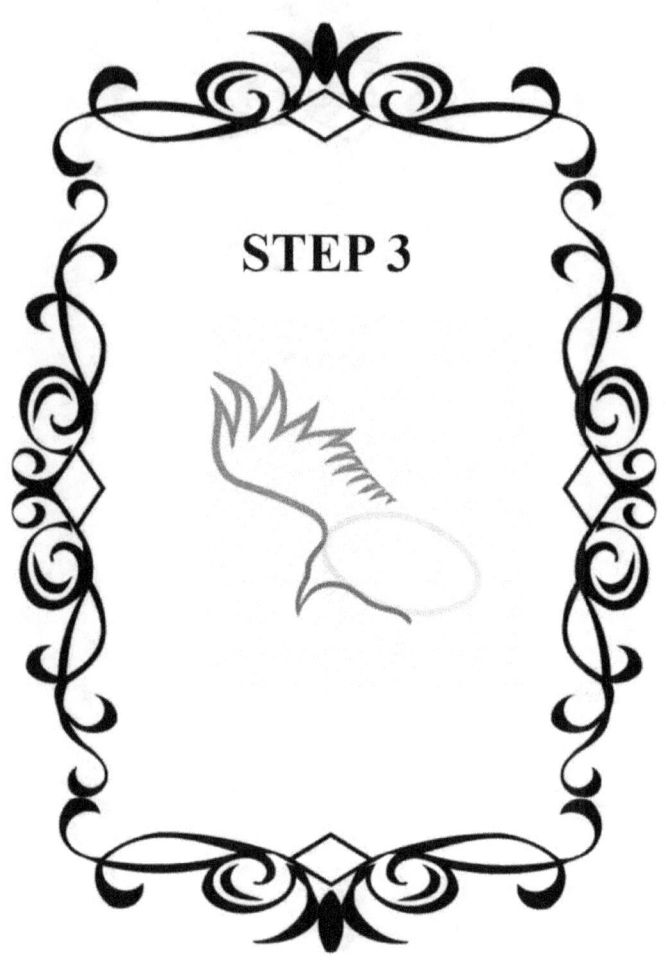

STEP 3

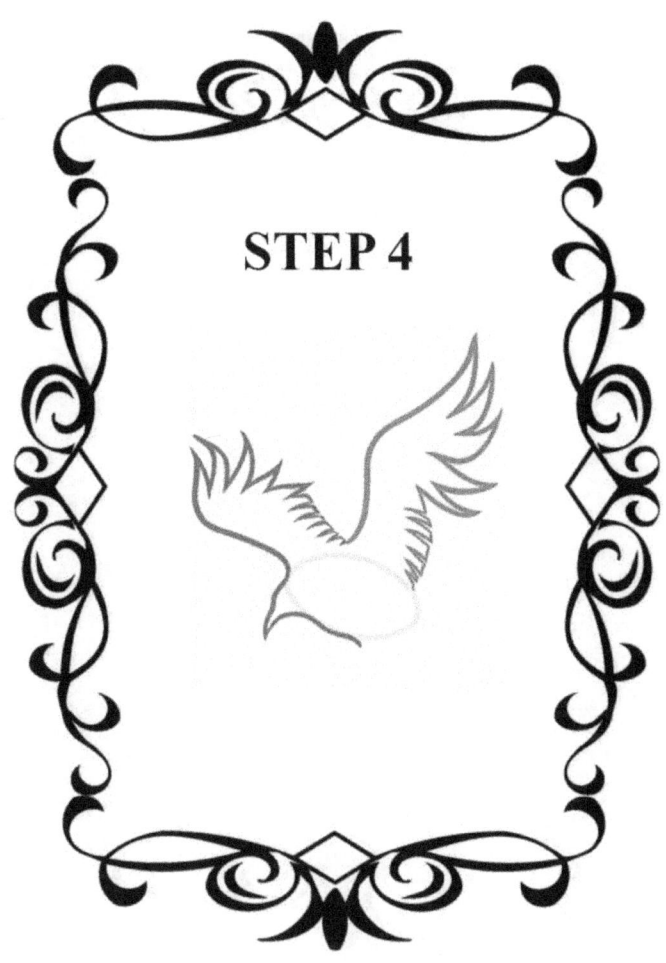

STEP 4

STEP 5

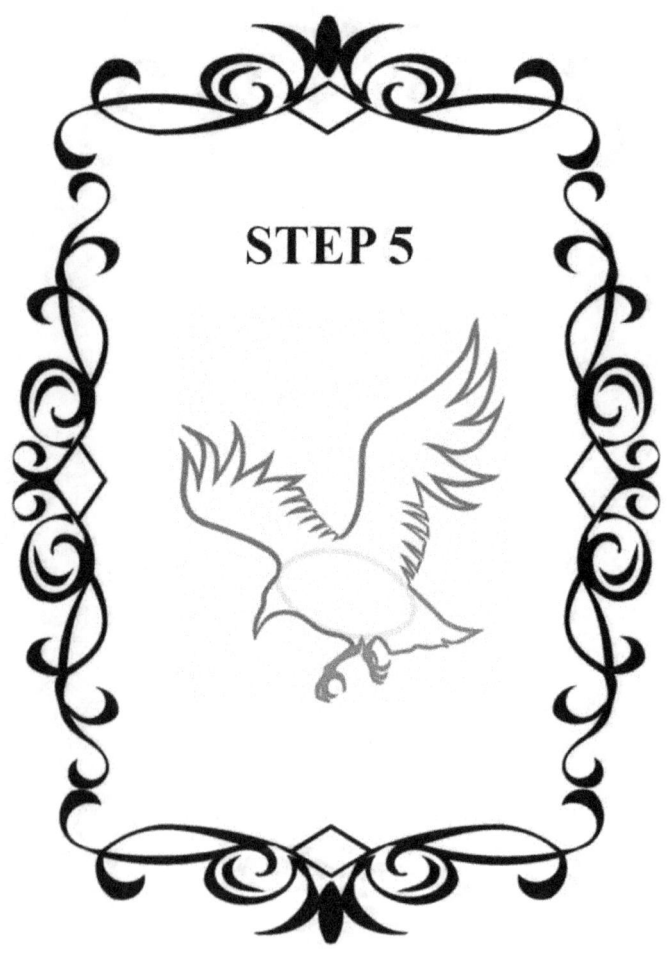

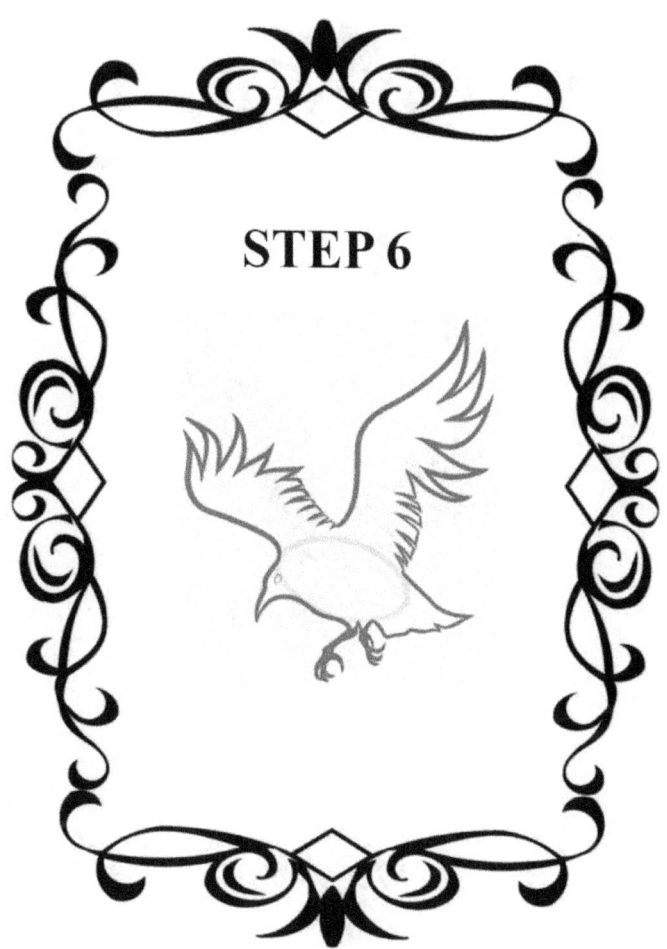

STEP 6

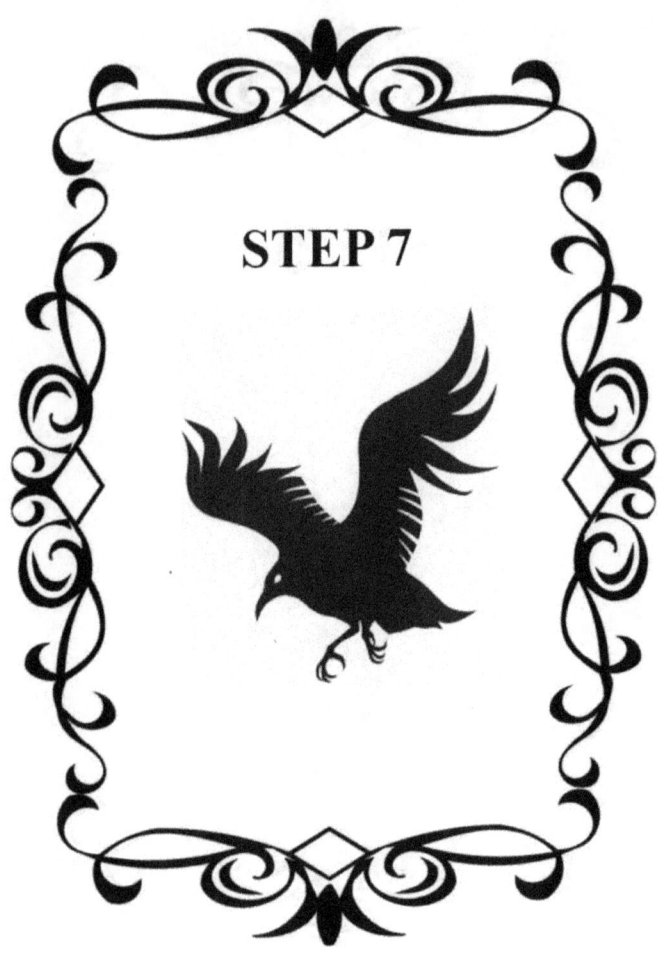

STEP 7

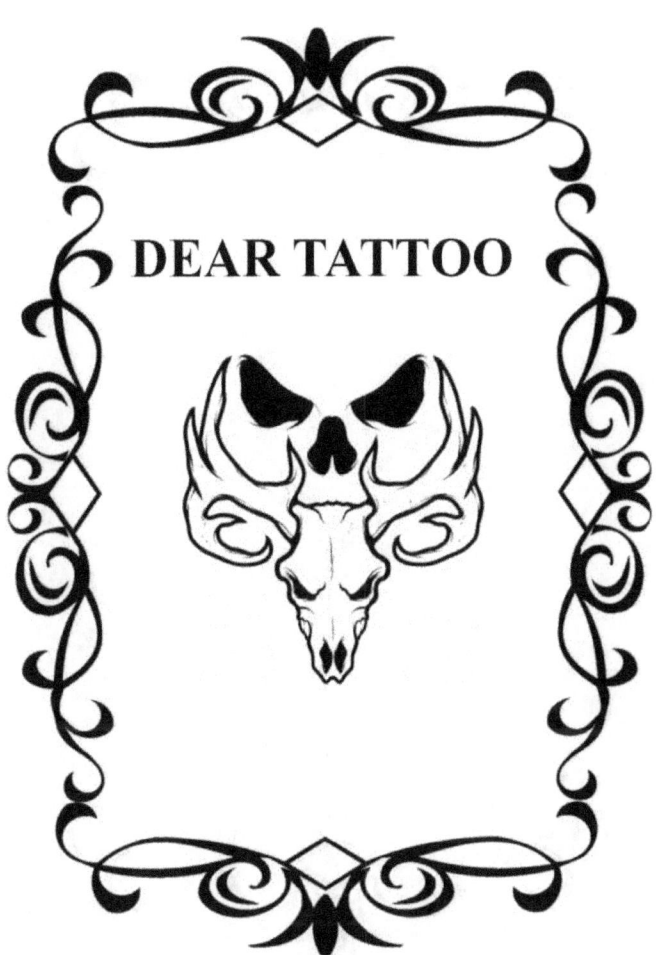

DEAR TATTOO

STEP 1

STEP 2

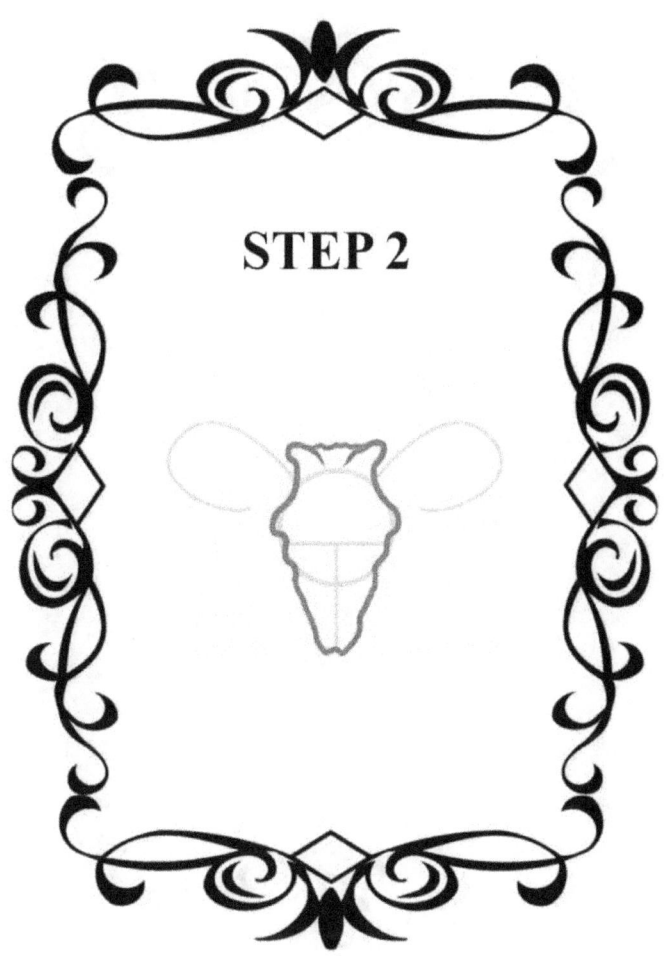

STEP 3

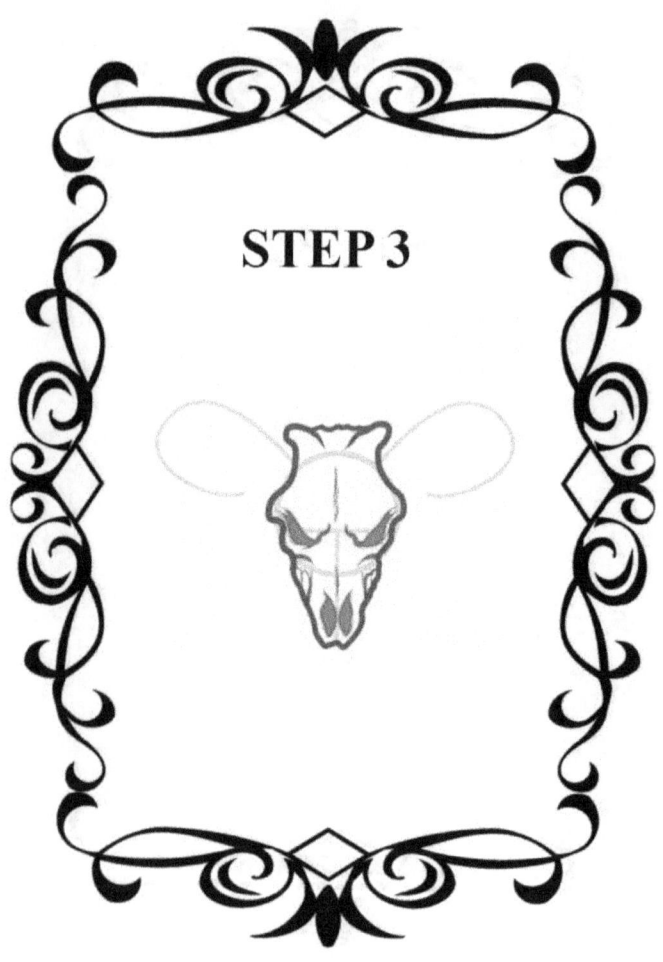

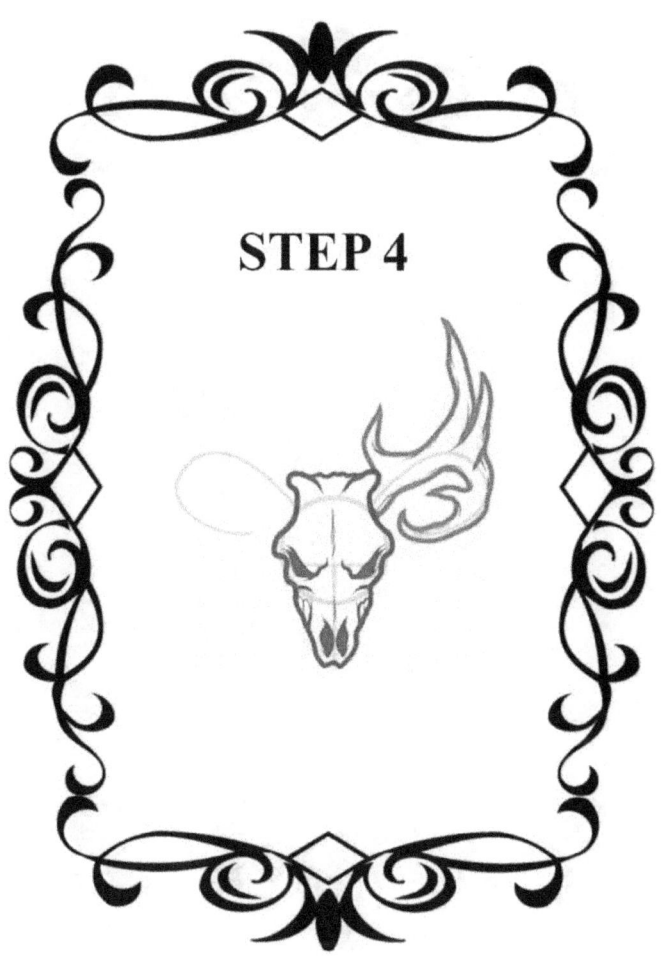

STEP 4

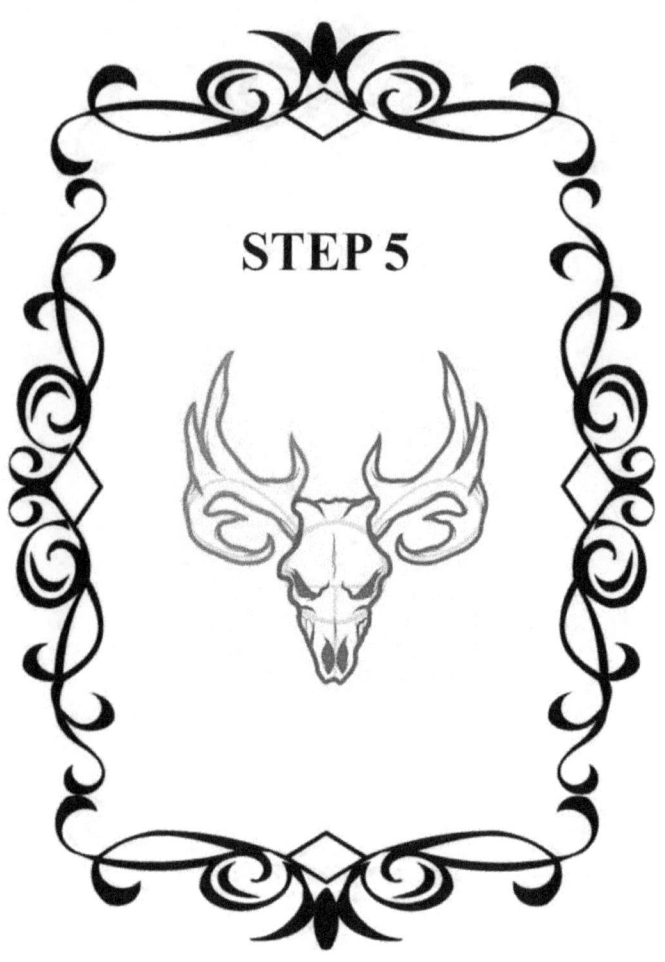

STEP 5

STEP 6

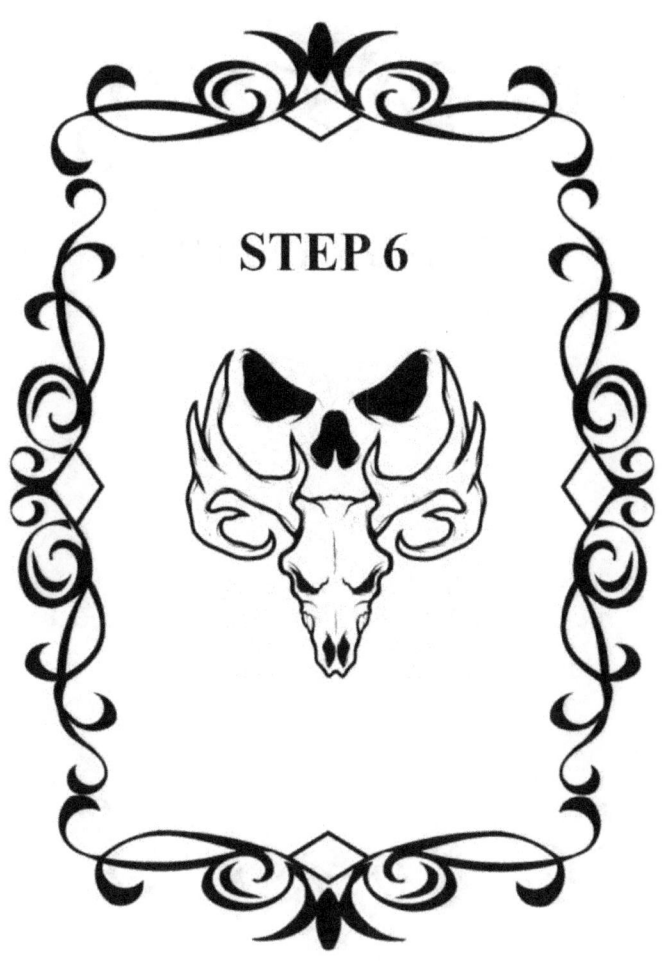

DOLPHIN TATTOO

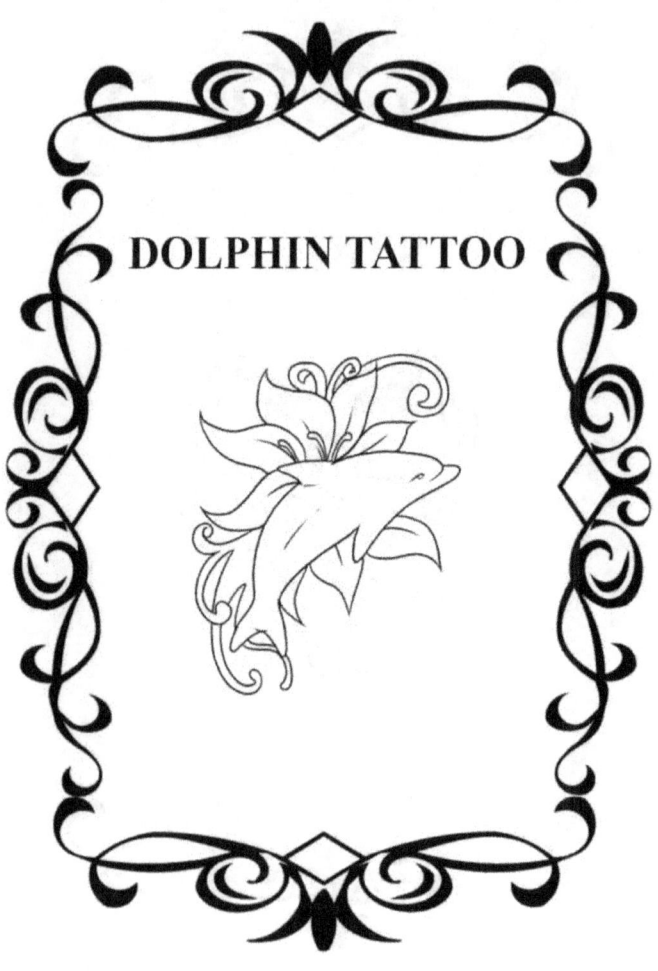

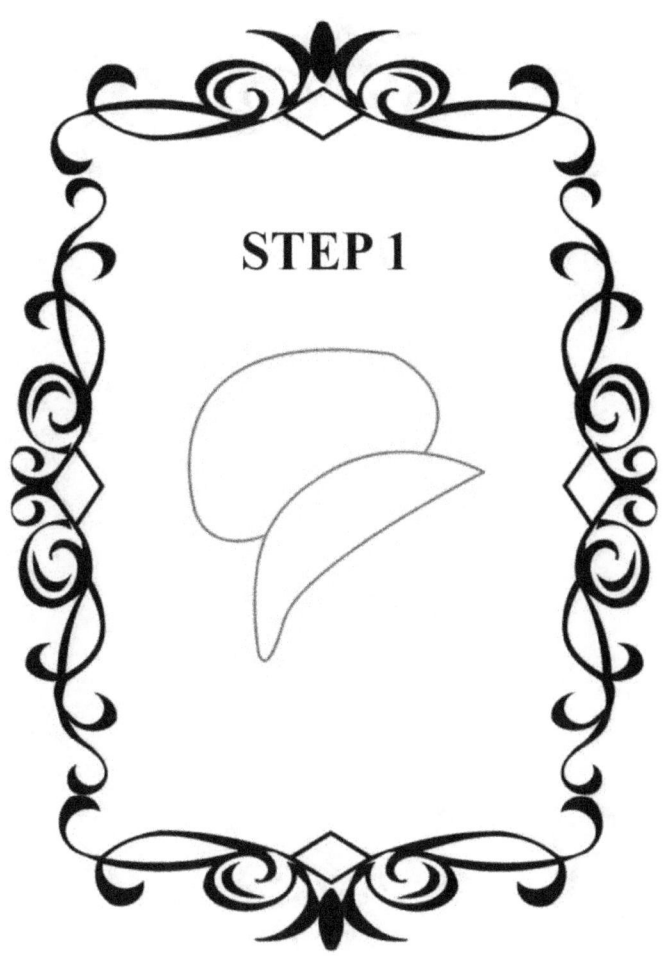

STEP 1

STEP 2

STEP 3

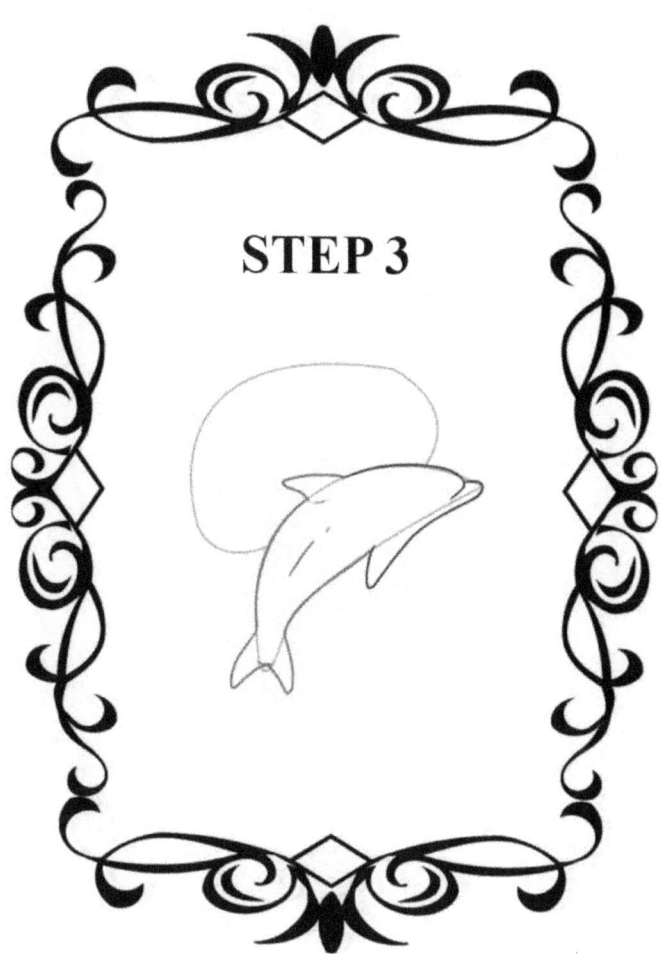

STEP 4

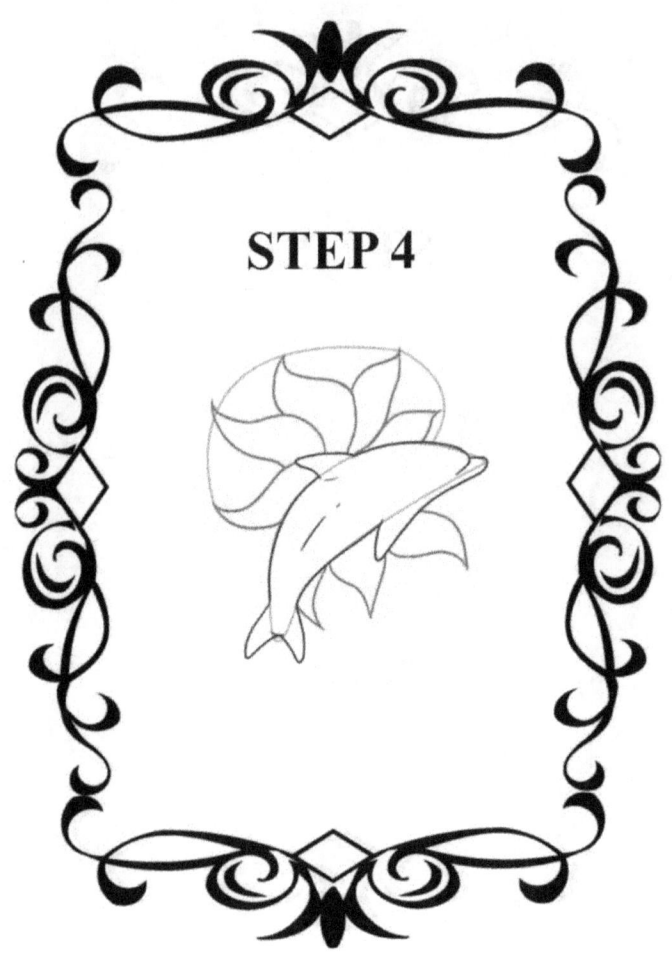

STEP 5

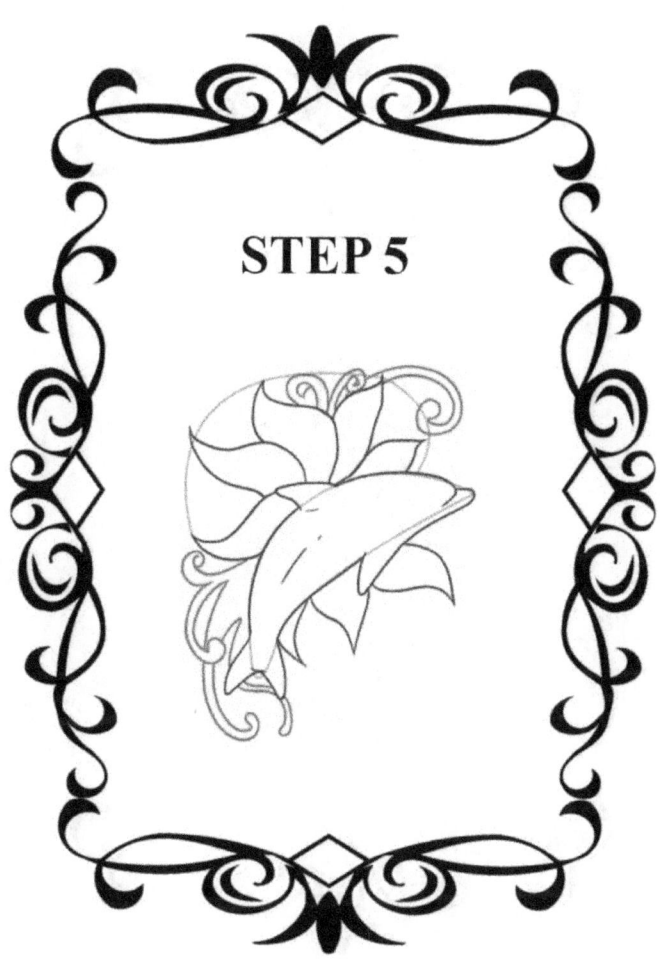

STEP 6

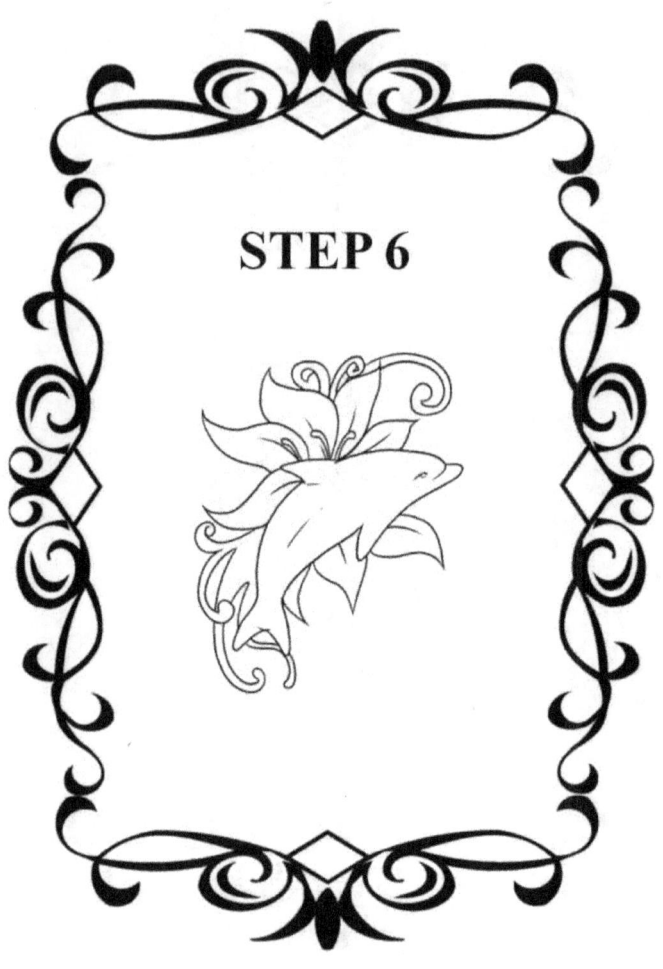

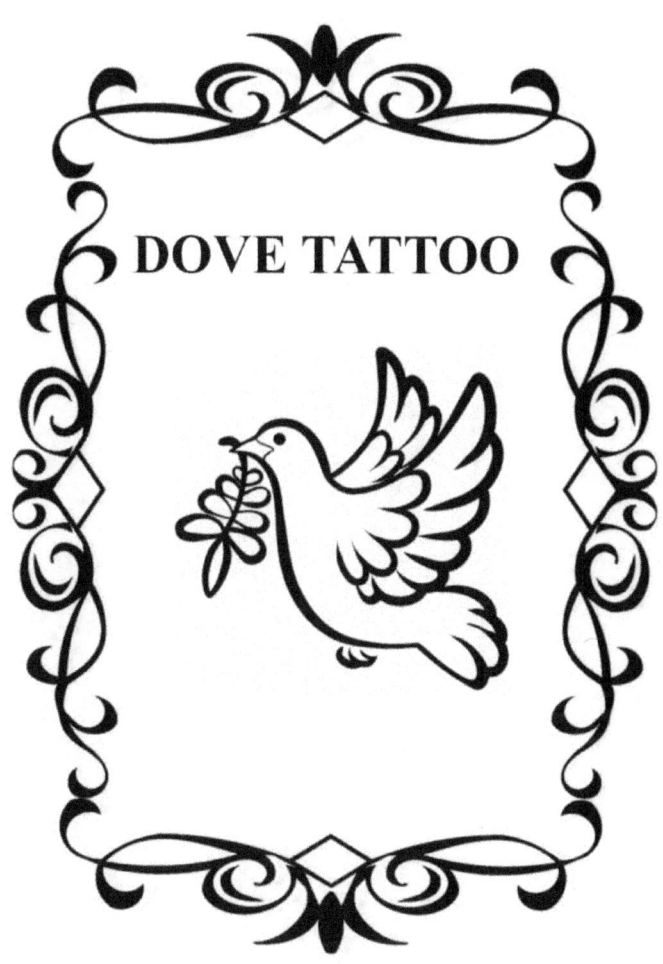

DOVE TATTOO

STEP 1

STEP 2

STEP 3

STEP 4

STEP 5

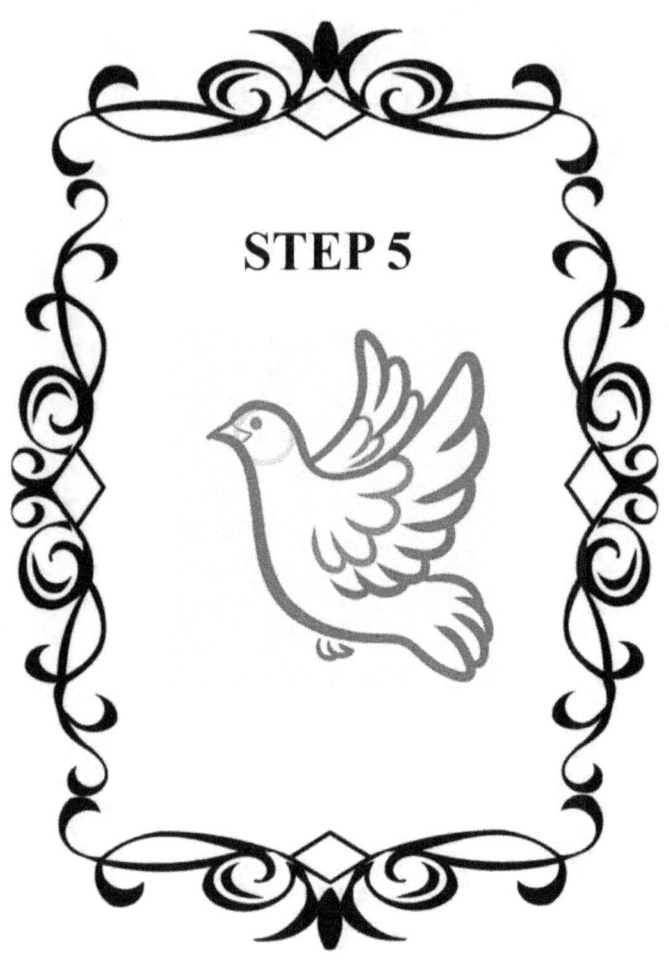

STEP 6

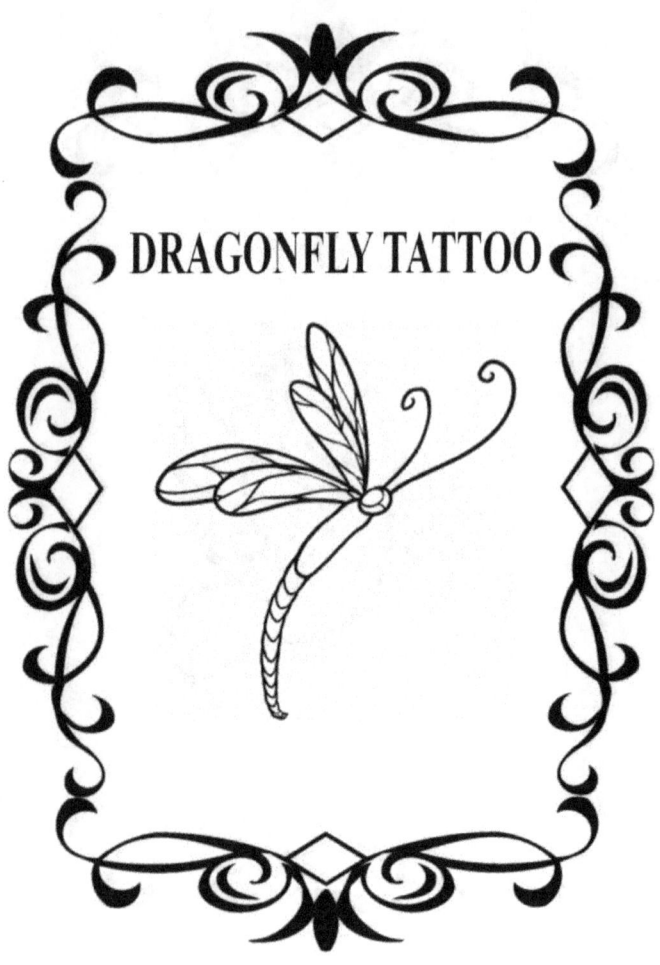

STEP 1

STEP 2

STEP 3

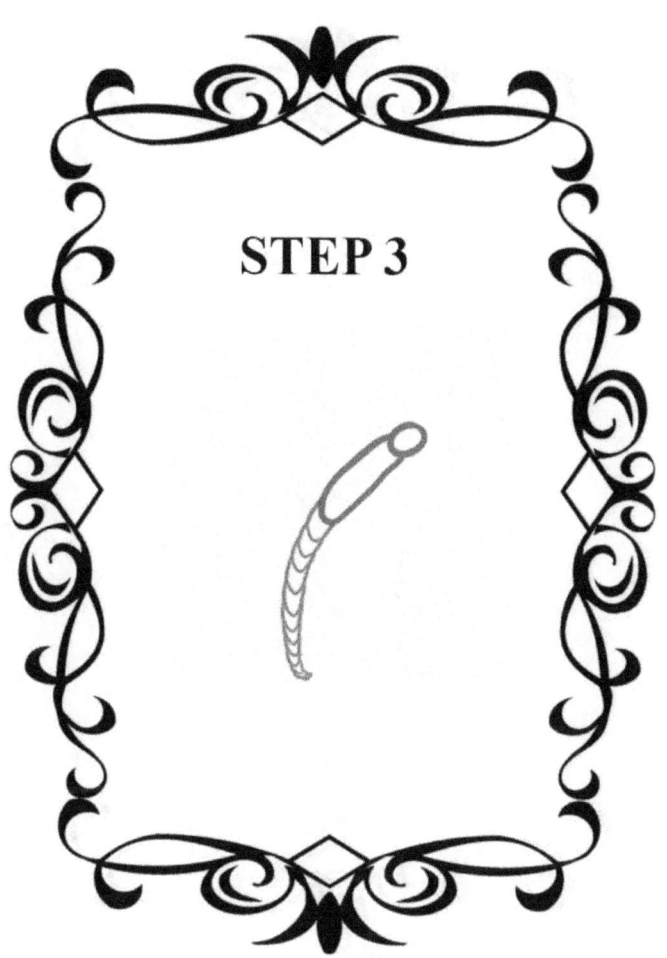

STEP 4

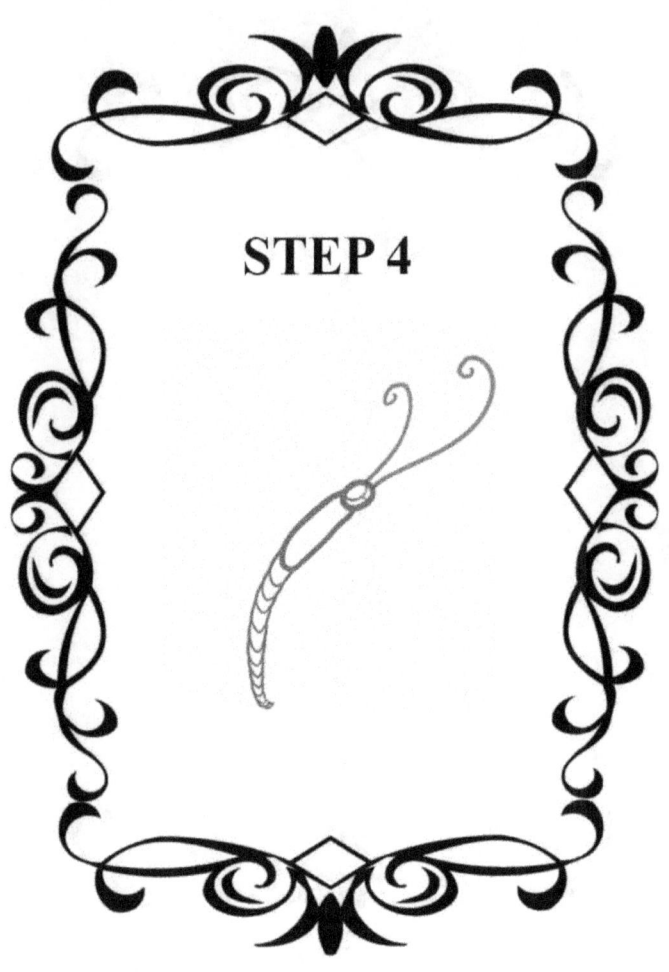

STEP 5

STEP 6

STEP 7

EAGLE TATTOO

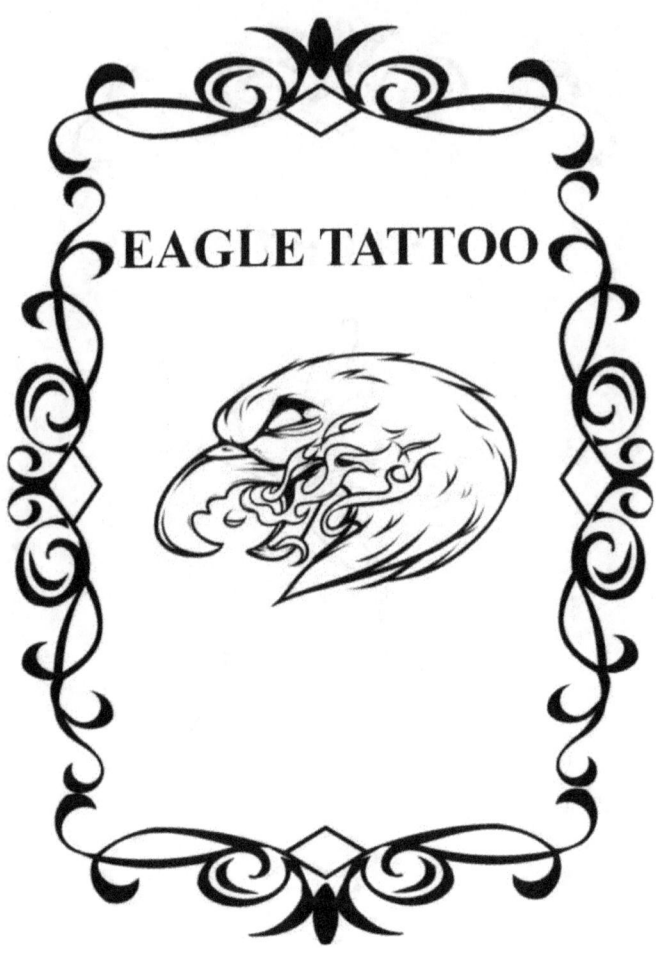

STEP 1

STEP 2

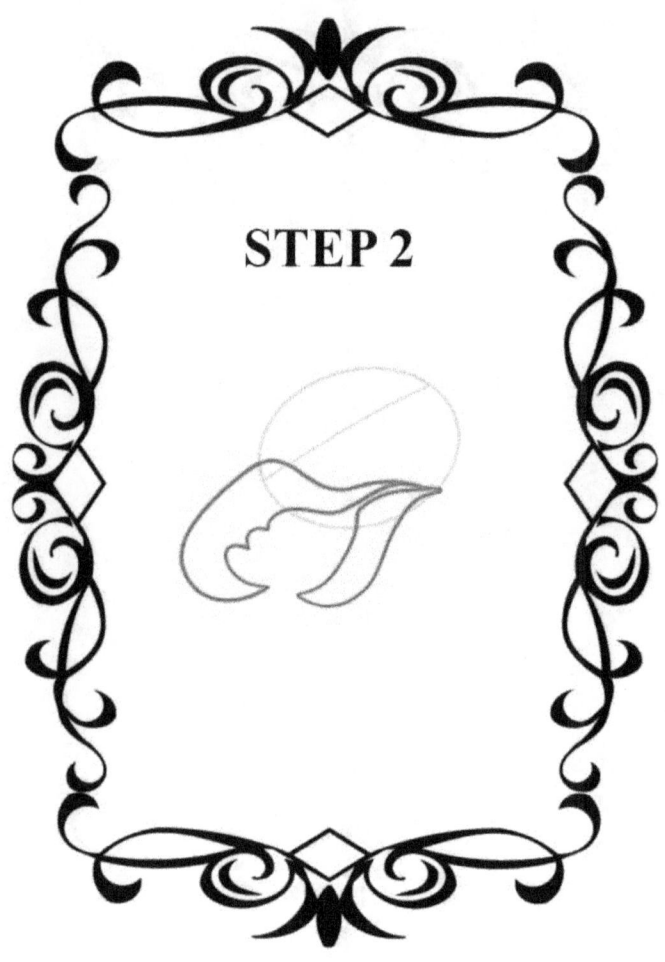

STEP 3

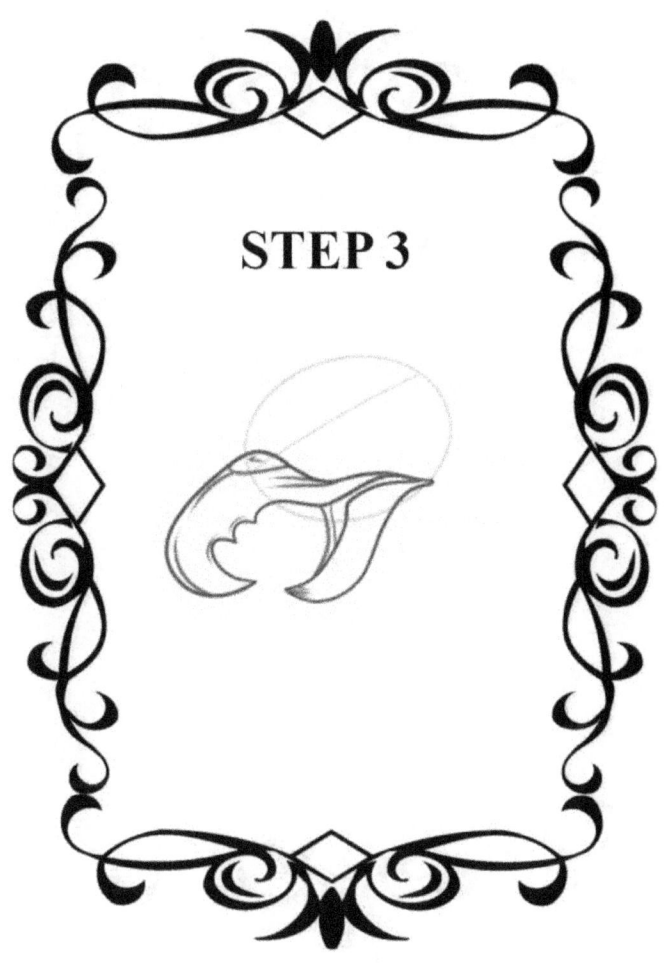

STEP 4

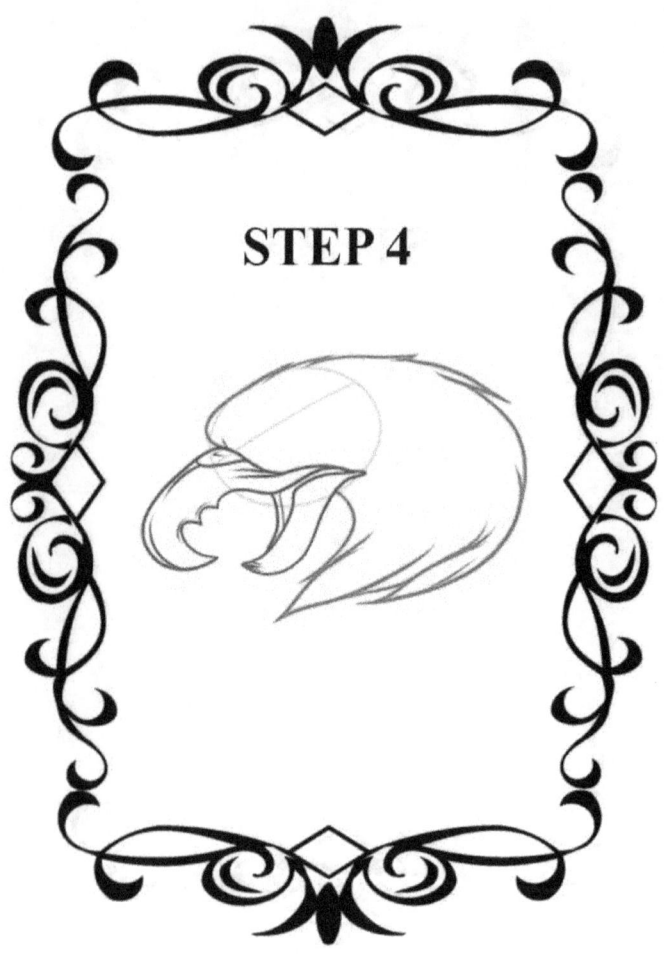

STEP 5

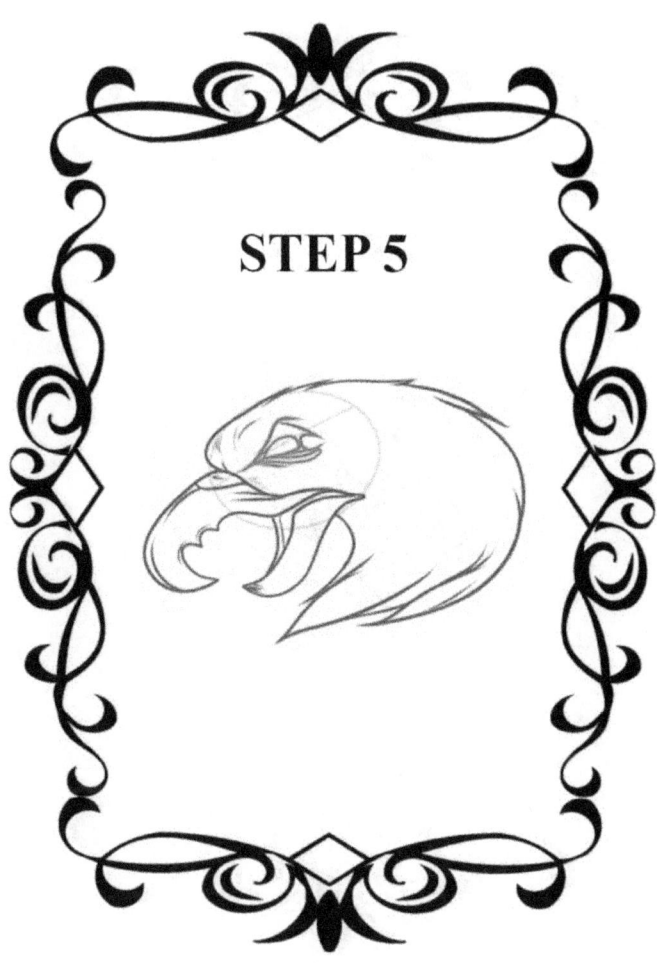

STEP 6

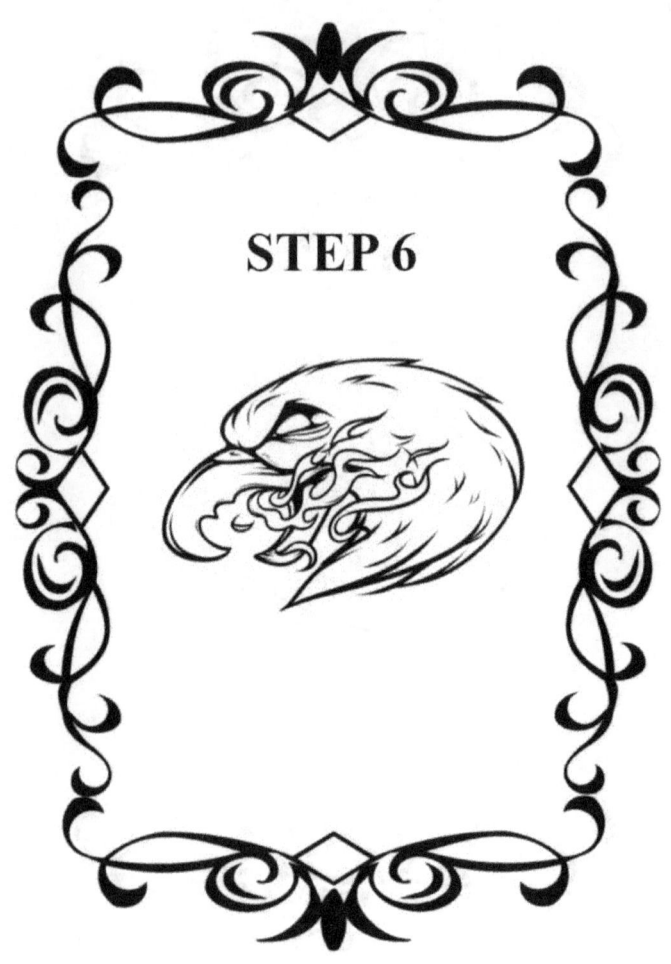

FISH TATTOO

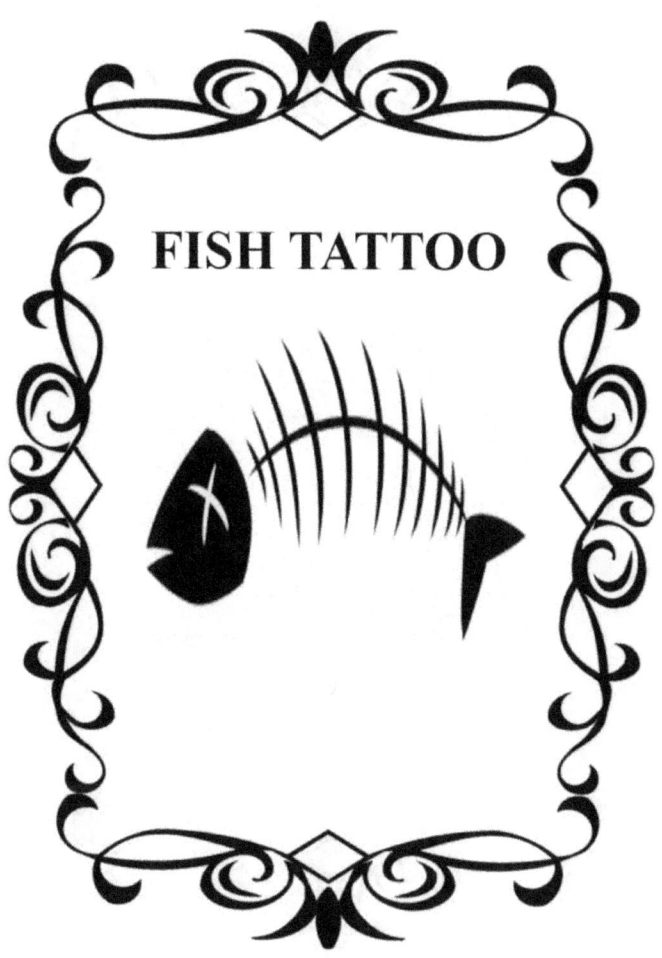

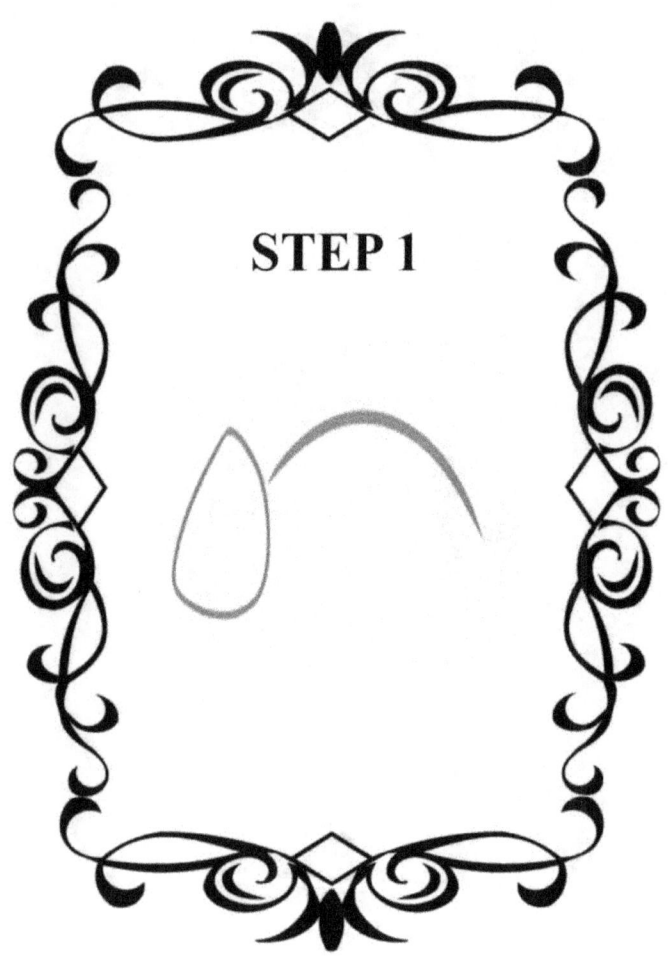

STEP 1

STEP 2

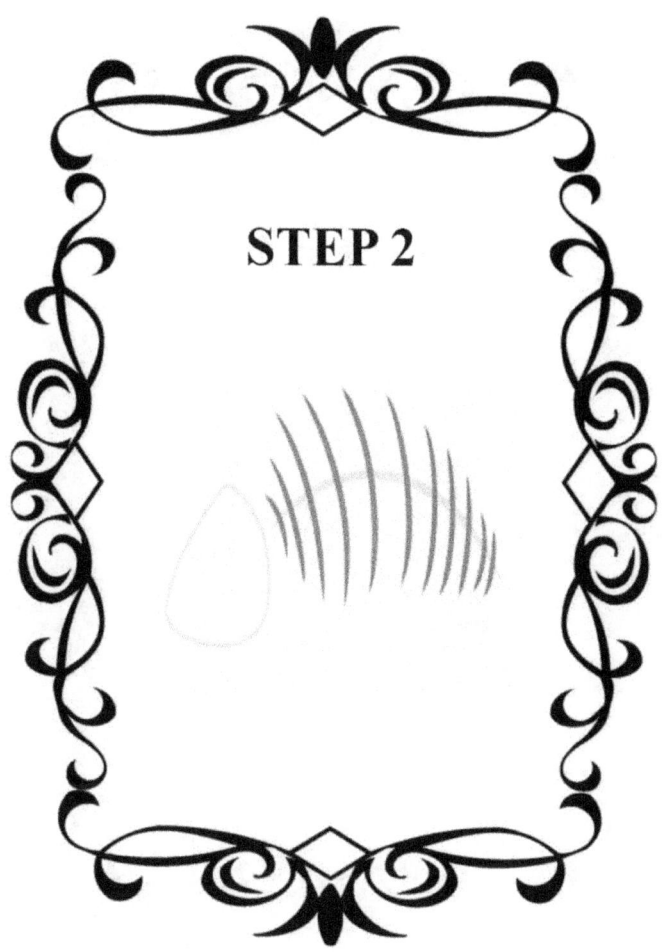

STEP 3

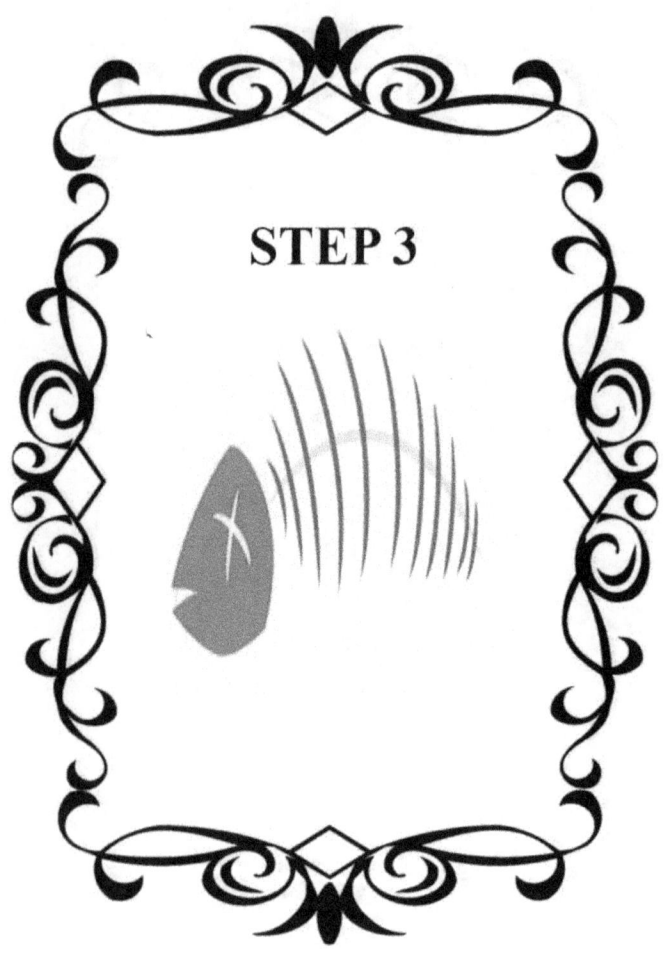

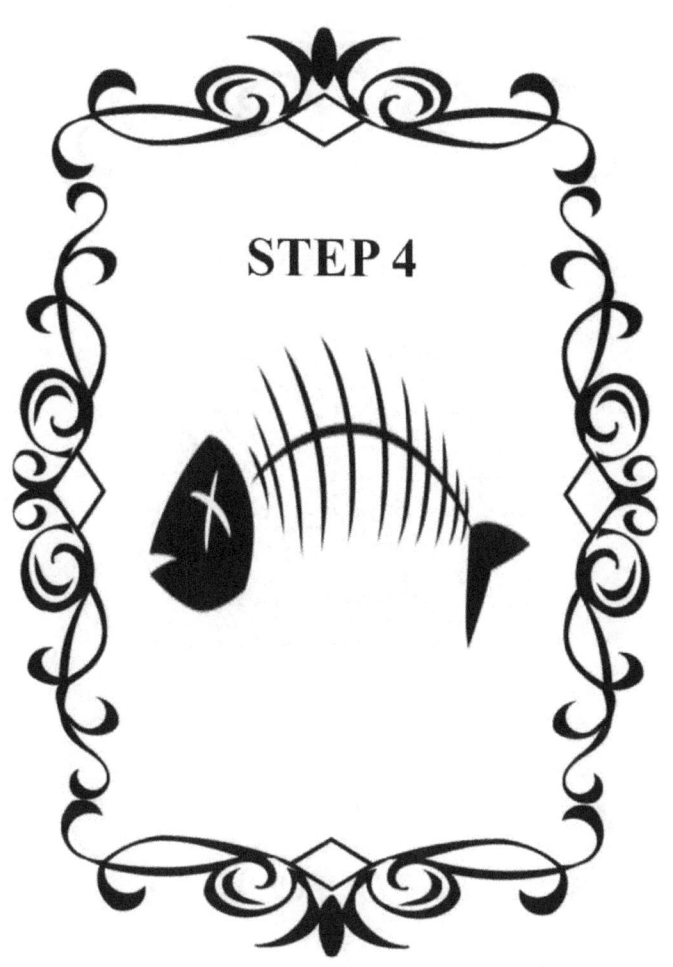

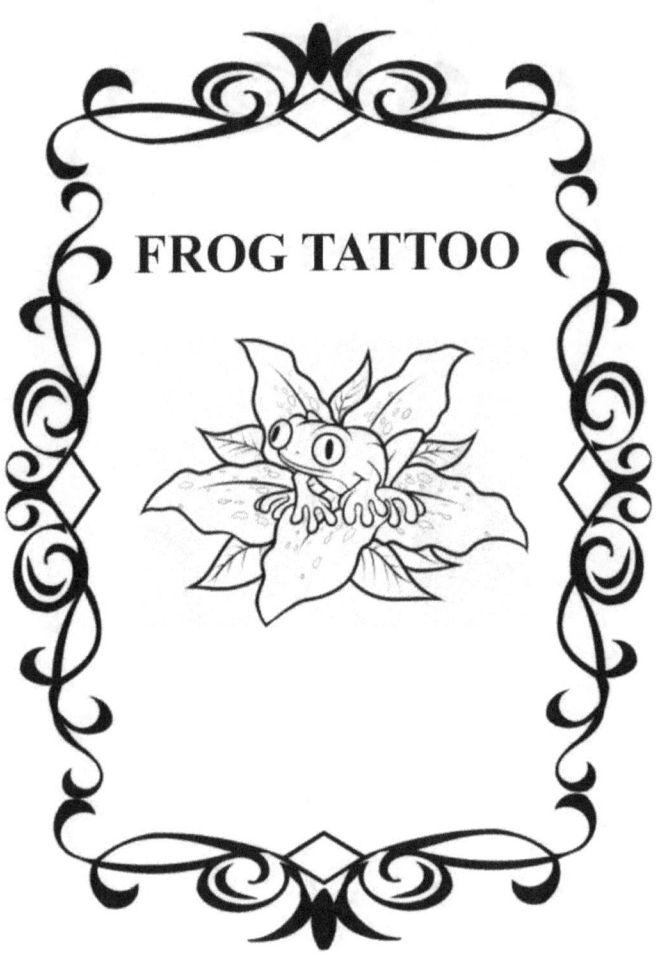

FROG TATTOO

STEP 1

STEP 2

STEP 3

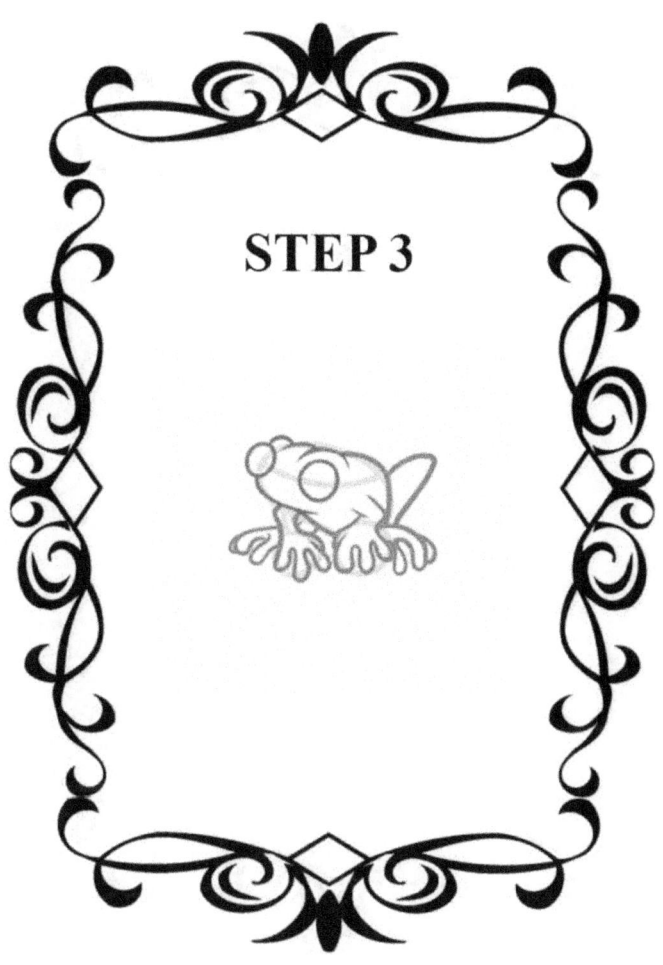

STEP 4

STEP 5

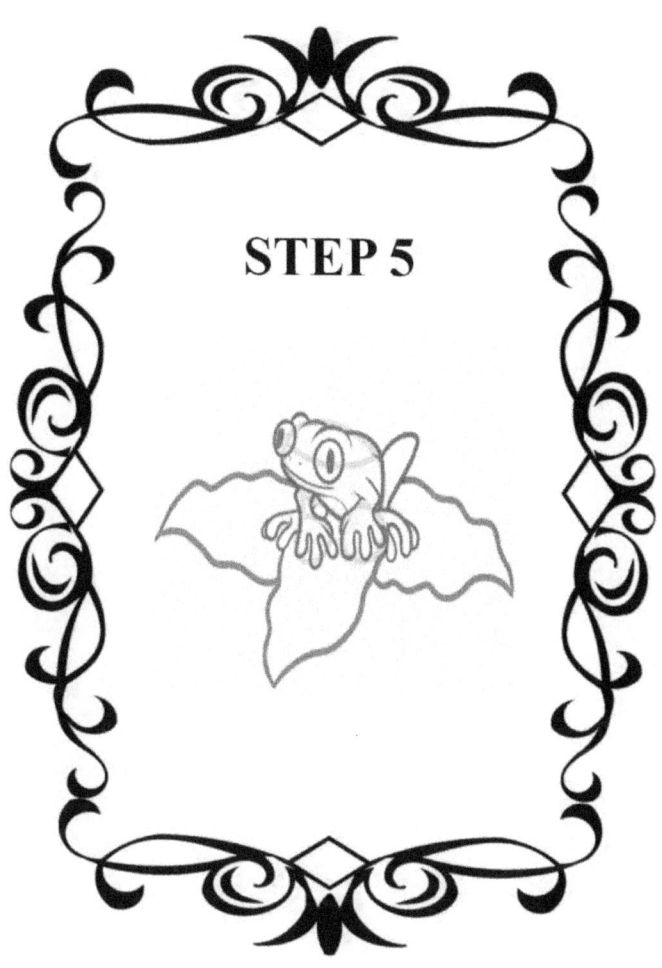

STEP 6

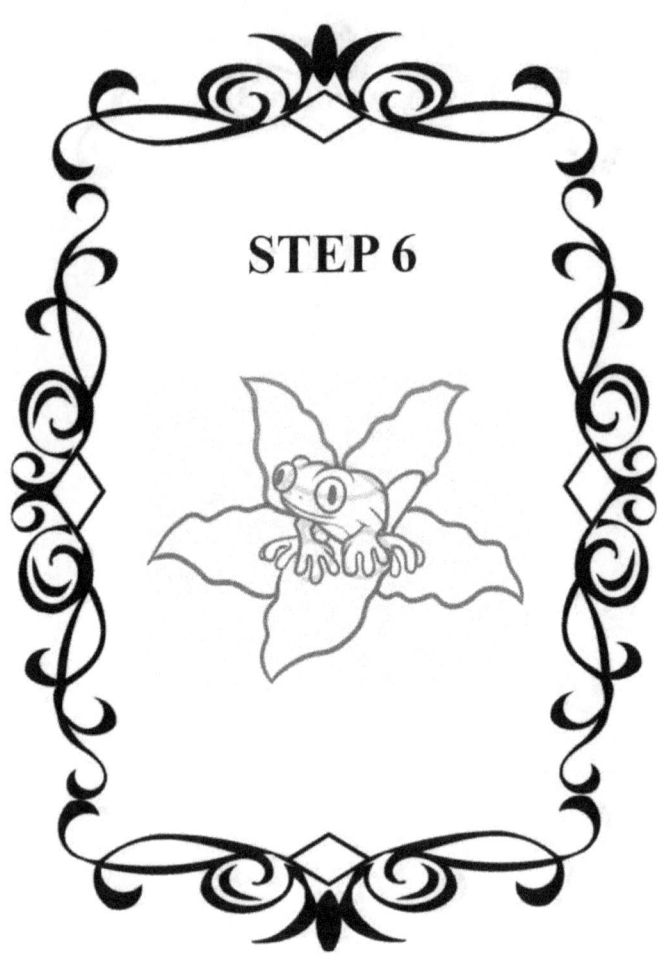

STEP 7

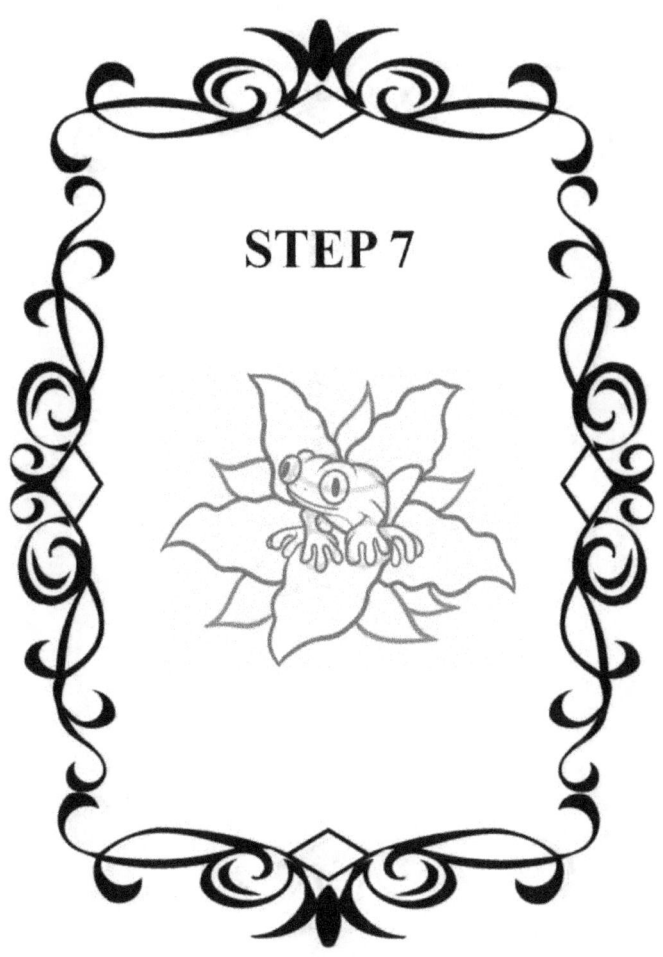

STEP 8

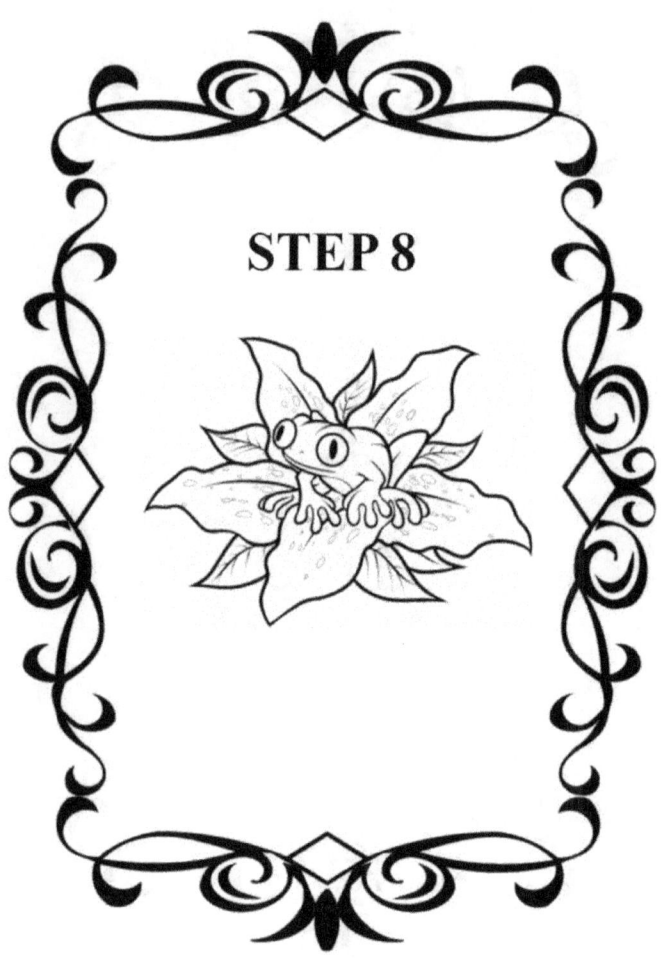

PITBULL TATTOO

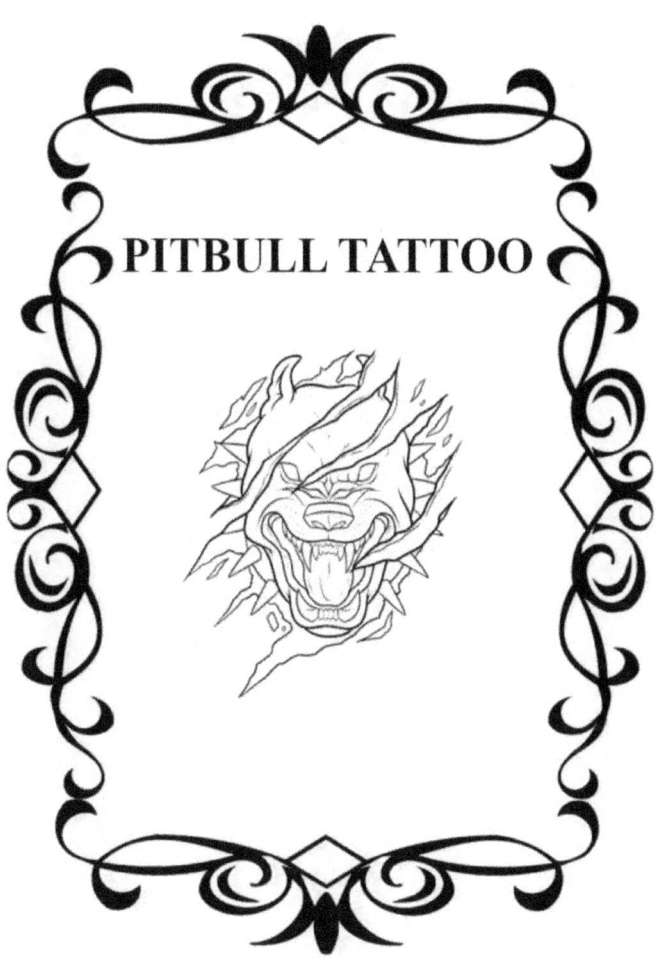

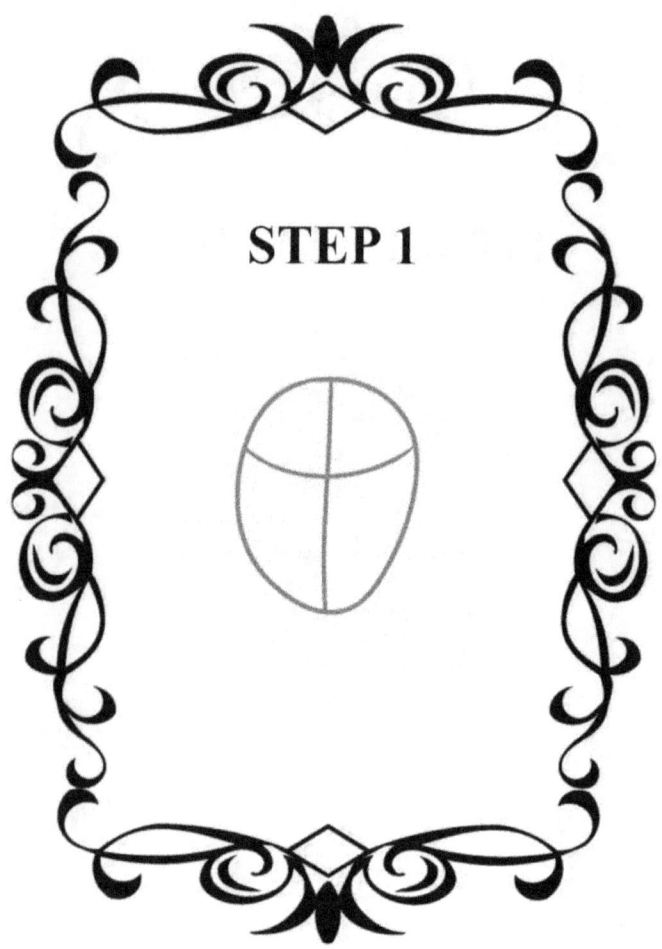

STEP 1

STEP 2

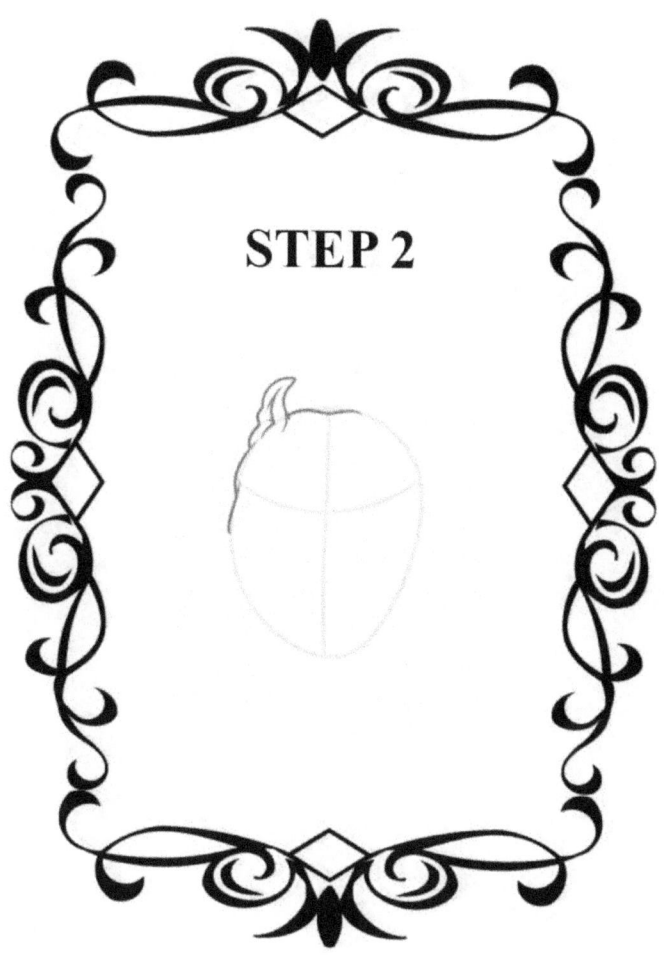

STEP 3

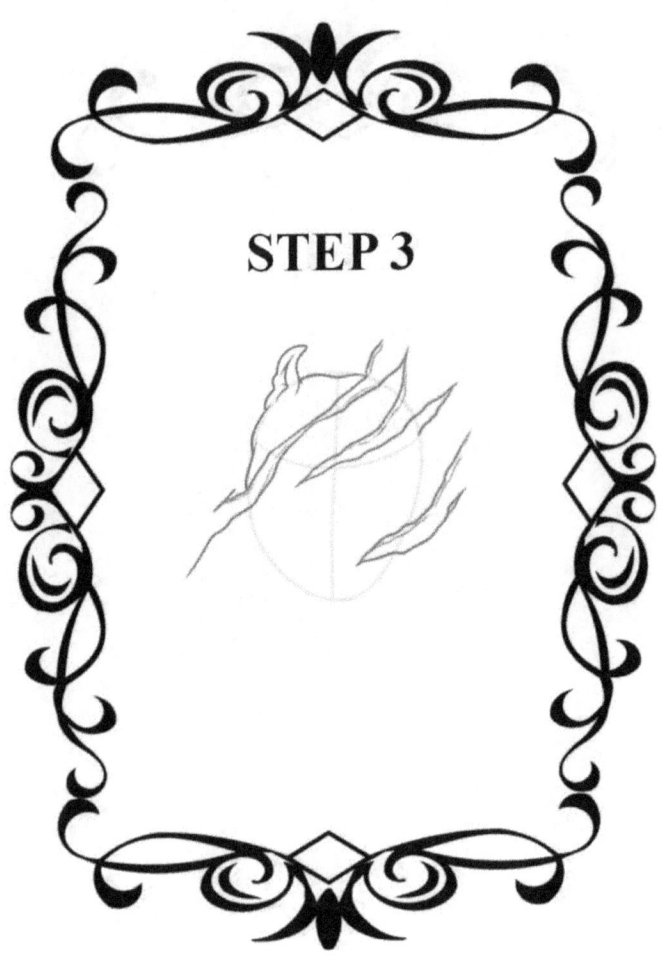

STEP 4

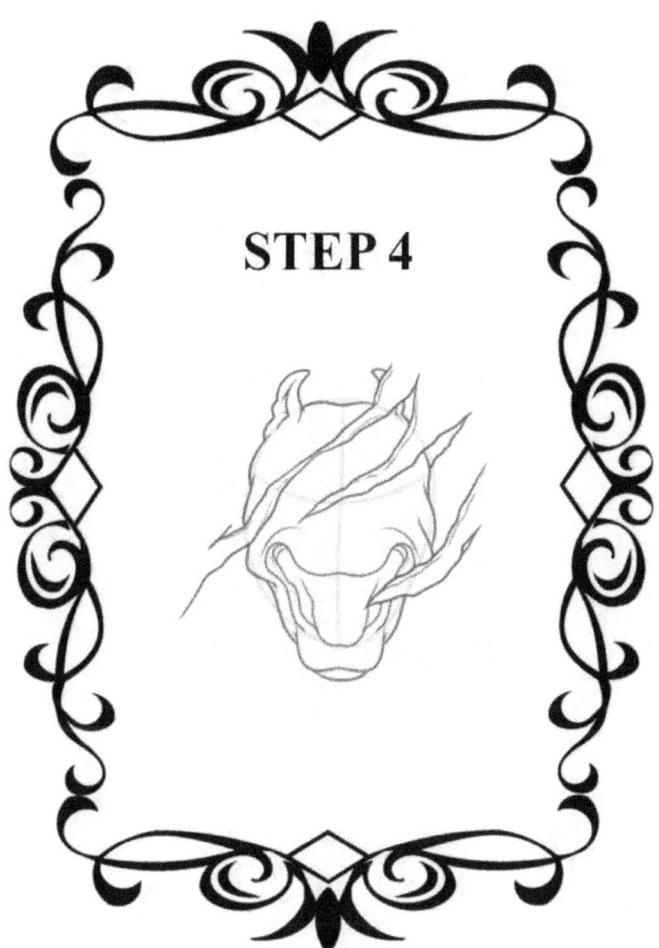

STEP 5

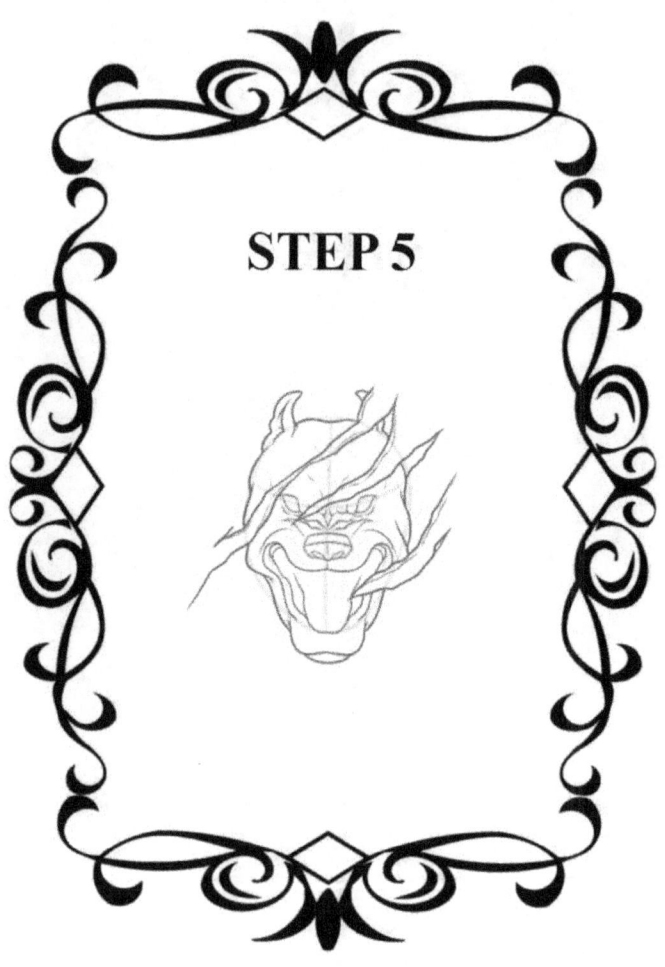

STEP 6

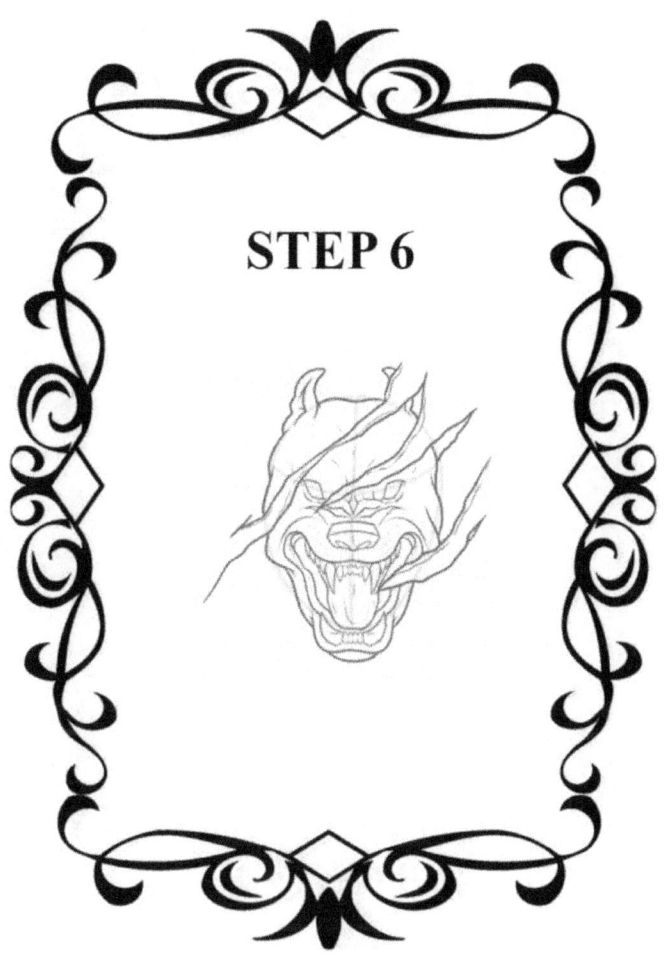

STEP 7

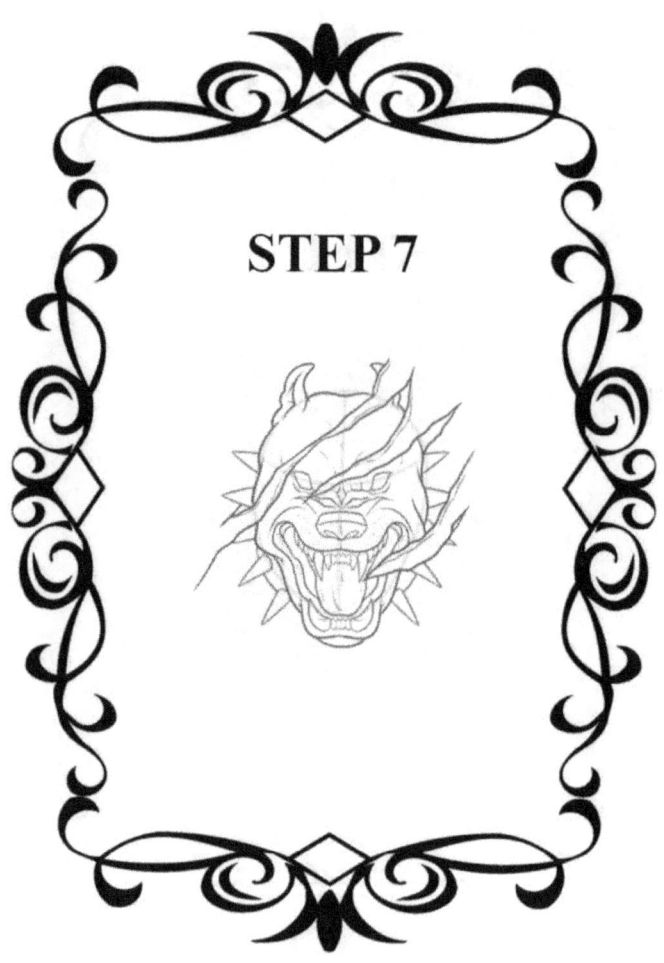

STEP 8

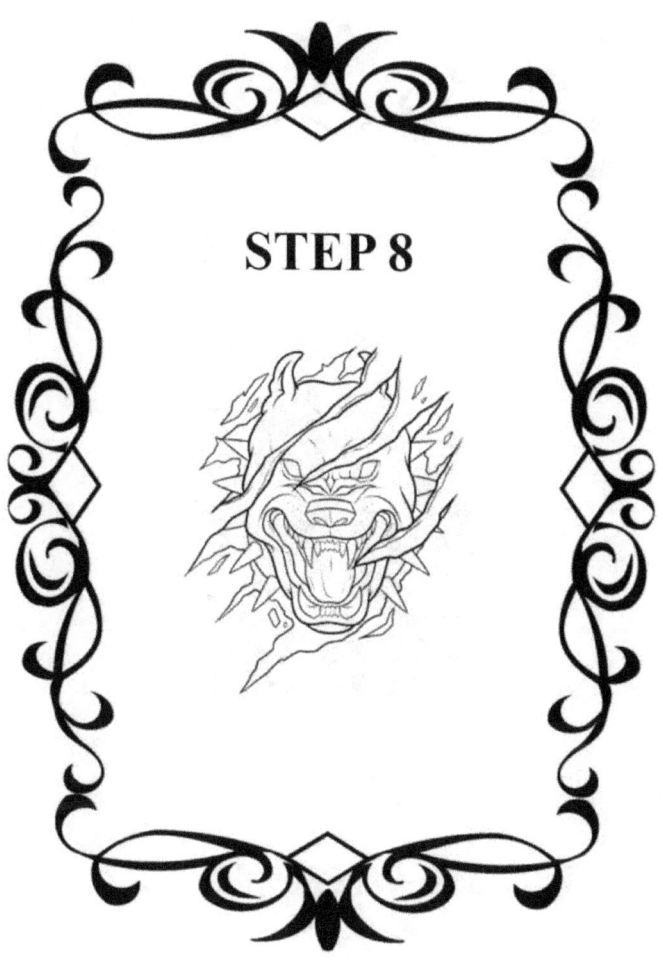

TRIBAL PAW

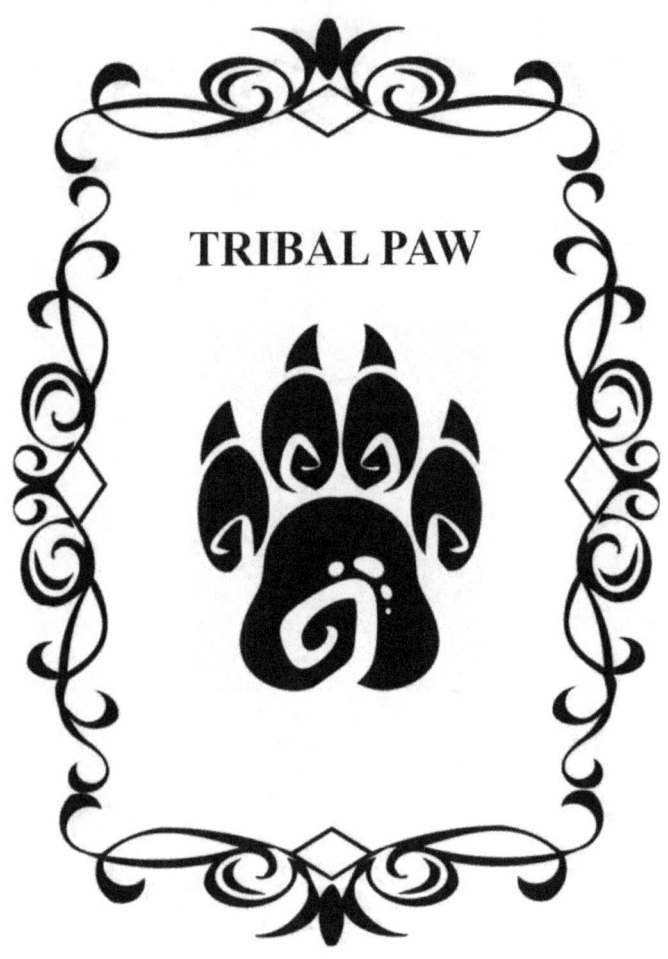

STEP 1

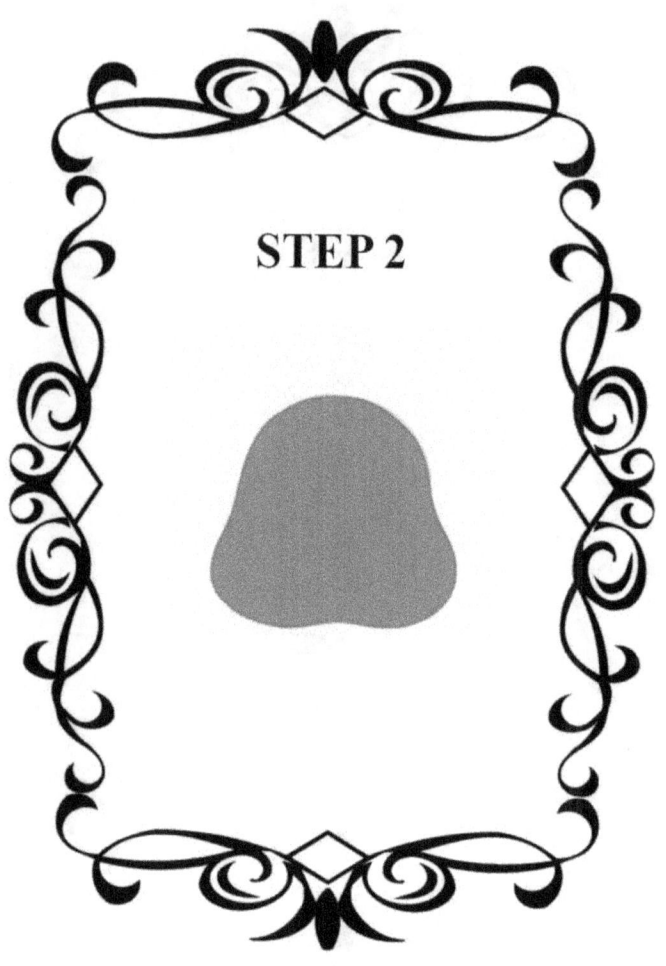

STEP 2

STEP 3

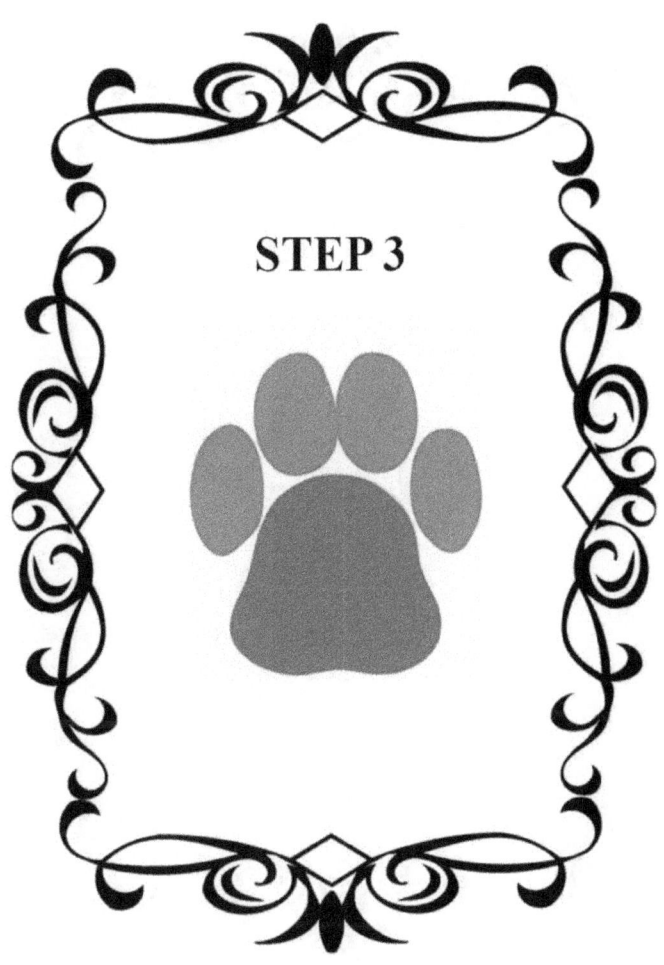

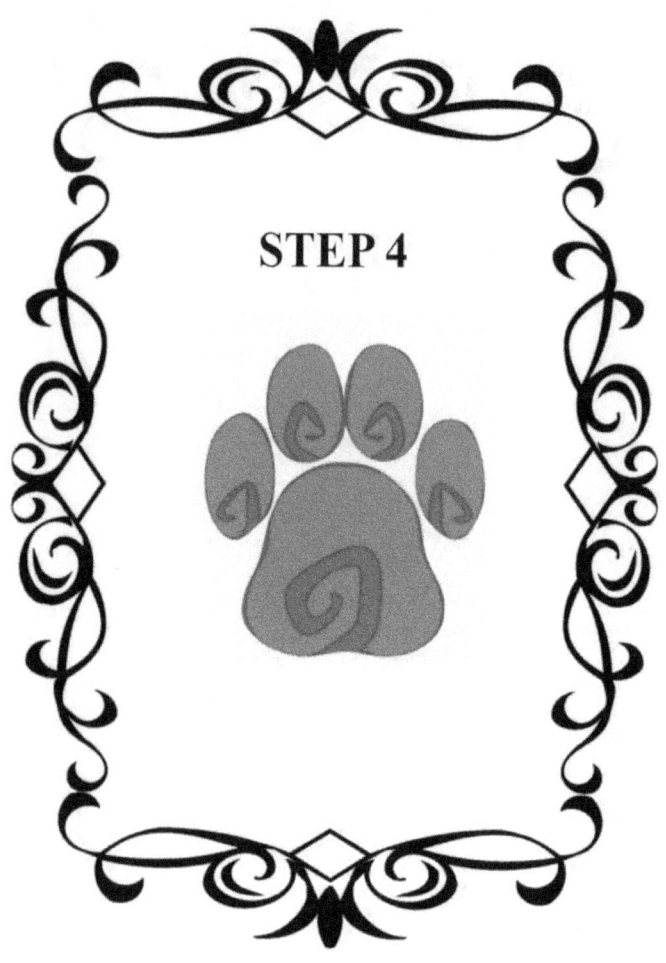

STEP 4

STEP 5

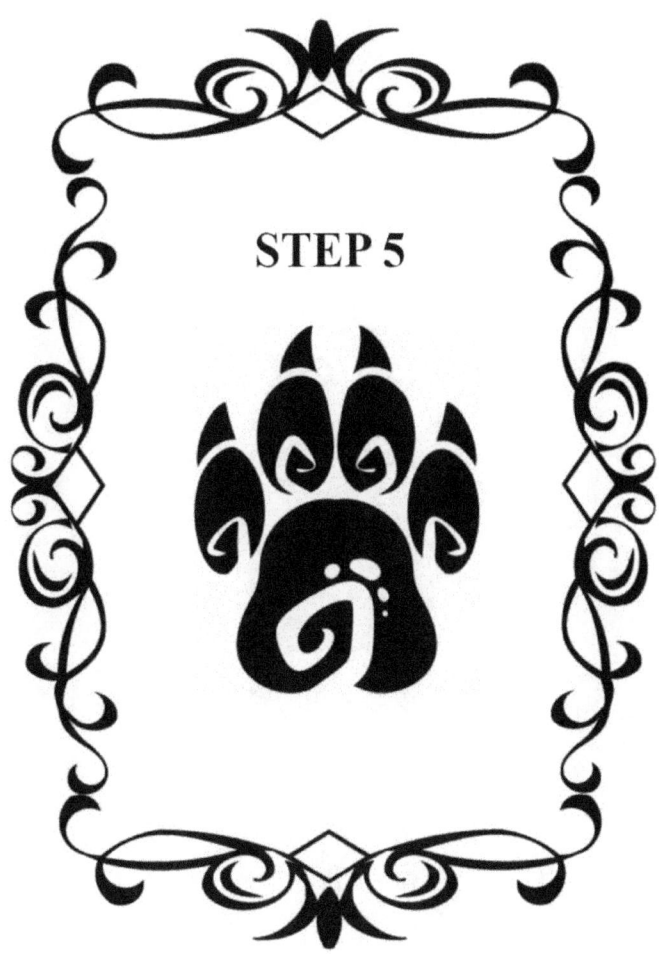

www.ingramcontent.com/pod-product-compliance
Lightning Source LLC
Chambersburg PA
CBHW071619170526
45166CB00003B/1114